Women's Konkatsu Tales

I Talk You Talk Press

Copyright © 2018 I Talk You Talk Press

ISBN: 978-4-907056-94-0

www.italkyoutalk.com

info@italkyoutalk.com

All rights reserved. No part of this publication may be resold, reproduced, stored in retrieval system, copied in any form or by any means, electronic, mechanical, photocopying, recording or otherwise transmitted without the prior written permission from the publisher. You must not circulate this publication in any format, online or otherwise.

This book contains true stories. All names and identifying details have been changed to protect the privacy of individuals.

Although the author and publisher have made every effort to ensure that the contents of this book were correct at press time, the author and publisher do not assume and hereby disclaim any liability to any party for any loss, damage, or disruption caused by errors or omissions, whether such errors or omissions result from negligence, accident, or any other cause.

Image copyright: © paylessimages #33737789 Standard License

CONTENTS

Introduction	1
One	2
Two	4
Three	6
Four	8
Five	10
Six	12
Seven	14
Eight	16
Thank You	18
About the Author	20

INTRODUCTION

"Konkatsu" is a Japanese word.
It means "searching for a marriage partner".

We asked many of our female friends in Japan about their search for a marriage partner. The women told us some very interesting stories. We chose eight of these stories for this book.

Some Japanese words are used in this book. The Japanese words are:
1. *o-miai* - an introductory meeting / a formal marriage interview
2. *o-nigiri* - rice ball
3. *ramen* - noodles
4. *bento* - lunch box
5. *tatami* - straw mats
6. *san* - Mr/Ms

ONE

A san (30) Hyogo Prefecture

A year ago, I joined an Internet dating site. The site is very popular in Japan. At first, I was nervous.

My friend said, "You should not join the dating site. Internet dating sites are very dangerous!"

However, the site has a very good system. Men cannot send me emails directly. First, they send emails to the site. Then, the site sends the emails to me. It is a very safe system.

I received many emails from men, but I didn't reply. The men were not my type. Some men were too old for me. Others lived in Tokyo. I wanted to stay in Hyogo. I didn't want to move to Tokyo, and I didn't want a long-distance relationship.

One day, I received an email from a man in Kobe, Hyogo. I checked his profile. He was thirty-five years old. He worked for an international company.

We exchanged emails for two months.

Then, he asked, "Would you like to have dinner together?"

I answered, "Yes, I would."

Before the date, I went to the beauty salon and I had a manicure. I also bought a new dress.

The date was at an Italian restaurant in Kobe. I was very nervous. I walked into the restaurant. The waiter took me to the table. The man was waiting for me.

We ordered a bottle of wine and some spaghetti and pizza. We talked for many hours. He asked me many questions. He was not shy.

I had a very nice time.

The next day, he sent me an email.

---*Thank you very much. I had a very nice time last night. Would you like to go out again next weekend?* ---

I replied:

---*Thank you very much. I had a very nice time, too. Yes, let's go out again next weekend.* ---

So, the next weekend, we went to a restaurant, and then we went to *karaoke*. I had a very good time.

Every weekend, we had a date. Sometimes we went to Osaka, but usually we went to a restaurant or movies or concerts around Kobe. We both liked restaurants, movies and music.

After six months, he asked me, "Will you marry me?"

I was very surprised and very happy. Of course, I said, "Yes!"

Now, I am planning my wedding.

I think joining the Internet dating site was a very good idea. Many people say, "Internet dating sites are dangerous." But I was very lucky. I met a very nice man and I found a husband!

TWO

M san (34) Okayama Prefecture

I live in Okayama. I work in an office. I want to get married, but I am very busy every day. So I don't have time to meet many men. Most of the men in my office are married. There are some single men in my office, but they are too young for me. They are around twenty-five years old.

I want to get married because I want to quit my job and also, my parents are worried about me. Last year, I joined an Internet dating site. Some men emailed me through the dating site, but I didn't reply. The men were not my type.

Two months ago, the dating site gave me a profile and a photograph of a man. He was forty-two and he worked for a big company. He was from Okayama, too. I thought he was handsome. We decided to meet.

We met at a coffee shop near Okayama Station at 7:30pm. We sat down.

The waitress brought the menu to our table.

She said, "What would you like?"

The man said, "Two coffees."

I was very shocked! I don't like coffee! I never drink coffee! He didn't look at the menu, and he didn't say, "What would you like to drink?"

I felt very angry.

The waitress brought the coffees to our table. She said, "Would you like anything else?"

He said, "Bring an ashtray!"

He started smoking. I hate smoking! He didn't ask me, "Is it okay if I smoke?"

He started to drink his coffee. I tried to drink my coffee too, but coffee is bad for my stomach. I felt sick. I only drank half the coffee.

He spoke about his job and his university for an hour. He didn't ask me about my job or my life. I was very bored and I wanted to go home.

When I arrived home, I felt very tired, sick and angry.

The man's actions were bad, but I think I was bad, too. I didn't say, "Wait a minute! I don't drink coffee! I'd like to drink tea!" Also, I didn't say, "Please don't smoke." In the future, I have to be stronger. I have to give my opinion strongly.

I am still a member of the dating site, and I am still looking for a husband. I haven't found a suitable man yet.

THREE

A san (27) Hiroshima Prefecture

Two years ago, I went to a singles party with two friends and three men. The party was at a restaurant in Hiroshima. My friend arranged the party.

The men were very nice. They worked for a large insurance company. They were around thirty years old. We had a very good time. We talked about many different things. We enjoyed eating and drinking.

I spoke to one man for a long time. He was sitting opposite me. His name was Yoshi. Yoshi was very funny and kind.

I said, "What do you like doing in your free time?"

He said, "I like hiking."

I said, "Oh, so do I!"

I was very happy. We had the same hobby. We talked about hiking courses and mountain climbing. My friend also spoke to Yoshi a lot. At the end of the night, we all exchanged email addresses.

The next day, I spoke to my friends about the party.

I said to my friends, "I think Yoshi is very nice. I'm going to email him today."

One of my friends said, "I also think Yoshi is very nice. I'm going to email him today, too!"

We both laughed. We both liked Yoshi!

Later, the men emailed us to say thank you. They had a good time, too.

I said to my friend, "Yoshi emailed me to say thank you."

She said, "He emailed me, too. But I'm very sorry."
I said, "Why are you sorry?"
She said, "Yoshi asked me to go on a date next week."
I said, "Oh, that's great!"

But really, I felt a little disappointed. I liked Yoshi, too, but he didn't ask me to go on a date. My friend went on a date with Yoshi. They had a good time, and they became a couple.

Now, my friend and Yoshi are married! Of course, I am very happy for them. On their wedding day, I was my friend's bridesmaid. I hope they have a wonderful life together!

Now I have a new boyfriend. He is one of Yoshi's hiking club friends. Yoshi introduced us a few months ago. We go hiking together on Sundays. He is thirty-two years old and he works for the city office in Hiroshima.

I like him very much. I would like to get married very soon and start a family, so I am waiting for him to propose!

FOUR

Y san (28) Tottori Prefecture

I live in a small village in Tottori. I am single. There are not many young men in my village. When I was younger, I went to university in Osaka, and I had a nice boyfriend. But after I graduated, my parents said, "Come back to Tottori!" So I came back to Tottori and I found a job in a small office.

My parents want me to marry a man from Tottori, and they want me to live in Tottori forever. They are very traditional. They arranged an *o-miai* introduction for me. Of course, I was not happy about this.

The go-between was my aunt – my father's older sister.

The man was from the next town. His family was very rich. They had a big house and a big company in the next town.

We met in a traditional Japanese food restaurant. My parents, his parents and my aunt also came to the meeting. I didn't want my parents to come. I don't think mothers and fathers usually go to *o-miai* meetings, but my father wanted to meet the man's mother and father because his family is very rich.

We introduced ourselves. While we were eating, his mother talked to my mother, and his father talked to my father. The man was very quiet. He didn't talk, and he didn't look at me. So, I asked the man some questions.

I asked, "What kind of food do you like?"

He looked at his mother.

His mother said, "He likes noodles."

I thought this was very strange. Why didn't he answer? Why did his mother answer?

I thought, *Maybe he is shy*.

After dinner, my parents said to me and the man, "We will go to a different room. You two have coffee together and talk."

I said, "Yes, OK."

Then, the man's mother said to him, "Are you okay alone? Would you like me to stay with you?"

I was very surprised. The man was thirty-four! Why did he need his mother?

We had coffee, but we didn't speak. He didn't ask me any questions, and I didn't ask him any questions. We only drank coffee.

When I arrived home, my mother said, "You should turn him down! Say 'no'! He will not be a strong husband!"

The next day, I called my aunt. She said, "The man's mother called. He is not interested. He doesn't want to see you."

I said "Good! I don't want to see him again either!"

I don't want to do another *o-miai* introduction meeting ever again. Now in Japan, *o-miai* introductions are not so common. Young people want to choose their own marriage partners. But in some villages, in the countryside, some people still do *o-miai*. I don't like it. I want to choose my own husband.

FIVE

H san (32) Hyogo Prefecture

I am single. I had a boyfriend, but we split up two years ago. Since then, I have been looking for a new boyfriend. I want to get married soon. Last year, my co-worker arranged a date for me. The man was her older brother's friend. He was thirty-six years old. I was very excited.

We met on a Friday night after work at a restaurant in Kobe. It was very busy. There were many people in the restaurant. We sat at the counter. We ordered some food and some drinks.

The man was very friendly. He was tall and he was wearing a nice suit. We talked a lot. I thought he was very nice. However, he liked eating and drinking very much. He ate very quickly! When I was talking, he ate most of the food! I wanted to eat something too, so I ordered some more food. Then, he ate that food too! Also, he ordered many drinks. I had two glasses of iced tea but he had six or seven beers.

At the end of the night, I was still very hungry! I didn't have chance to eat much food. The waiter brought the bill. It was around 12,000 yen.

I thought that I should pay 4,000 yen, and he should pay 8,000 yen because he ate most of the food and he drank a lot.

However, he said to me, "Let's split the bill. 50-50!"

I was very shocked, but I said, "OK."

So, I paid 6,000 yen.

Later, on the way home, I went to a convenience store and I

bought an *o-nigiri* rice ball and some *ramen* noodles because I was so hungry!

The next day, the man sent me an email.

The email said, "I had a good time last night. Let's go out again. Are you free next Saturday?"

I turned him down. I said 'no'. I thought he was a nice man, but he ate so much! At that time, my salary was not so high. I thought, If I date him, I will need a lot of money! And, I will be very hungry!

On Monday, my co-worker asked, "How was your date?"

I said "It was very nice, but he isn't my type!" I didn't tell her the truth!

SIX

S san (33) Iwami area, Shimane Prefecture

I really want to get married. Also, my parents are very worried about me because I am not married. Every day, my mother says, "Please find a man! You have to get married!"

Last year, my friend arranged a date for me with her older brother. Her older brother was forty years old. He had never had a girlfriend in his life.

I didn't want to go on a date with him, but I couldn't say 'no' to my friend. She also wanted her brother to get married.

We met for lunch at a Japanese restaurant. My friend, his sister, came too. The man worked in a small factory in the town.

On the date, the man did not say anything! He didn't look at me. He didn't talk to me! He didn't even talk to his sister! All the time, he looked at the food on the table. I couldn't relax. I felt very tense. So, I couldn't eat much food.

I thought, *Maybe he is shy because his sister is here.*

I asked the man about his job. I asked, "How is your job? Is it hard? Is it busy?"

He said, "Yes."

I asked, "Yes? Yes what? Yes, it is hard? Or, yes it is busy?"

He answered, "Yes."

I asked, "Do you like your job?"

He said, "Yes."

That was all. He didn't say anything else, and he didn't ask me any questions. I felt very tired. I wanted to go home.

After lunch, my friend said, "Why don't you two go for a drive together?"

I didn't want to go for a drive with him, but I couldn't say 'no' to my friend.

So, we went for a drive in his car. He didn't talk. I tried to start a conversation again.

I said, "It is nice weather, today."

He said, "Yes."

I asked, "What are your hobbies?"

He said, "Nothing special."

I asked, "Do you like music?"

He said, "No."

I asked, "Do you have any questions for me?"

He said, "No."

I was very angry and tired.

So I said, "I have one more question. Can you take me home? Now?!"

He said, "Yes."

He took me home.

I said, "Thank you."

I walked into my house. I went to my bedroom and called my friend.

My friend asked, "How was it? Did you talk?"

I said, "No, we didn't. I'm sorry, but I don't want to see him again. He is not my type."

"It's okay," said my friend. "I understand. He is too quiet for you!"

So, I am still looking for a marriage partner. I want to meet a friendly man with good communication skills. I hope I can find him soon. I want to make my parents happy.

SEVEN

K san (32) Okayama Prefecture

When I was thirty, my grandmother arranged an *o-miai* meeting for me. The man was her neighbor's grandson. He was thirty-one.

We had the *o-miai* meeting in a hotel restaurant. My mother and grandmother, and his mother and grandmother also came to the meeting.

I wore a kimono. I didn't want to wear a kimono, but my grandmother said, "You must wear a kimono!"

The man was very nice. He was a prefectural office worker in Okayama. He was not shy. He talked a lot. I liked him, but there was a big problem... his mother.

His mother asked me many questions. She asked me about my job and my life. It was like a job interview!

When she asked me questions, she didn't smile at all. She was scary.

She asked, "Can you cook?"

I said, "A little."

She said, "A little? Only a little?" She didn't look happy.

Then, she asked, "Can you clean?"

I said, "Yes, of course."

She said, "Good!"

After the meeting, I went home and spoke to my mother.

My mother said, "If you marry that man, you will have to live with his mother. You will be very tired and you will have much stress."

I liked the man very much, but I was worried about his mother.

The next day, I called my grandmother.

I said to my grandmother, "I am very sorry. He is a nice man, but I cannot marry him."

My grandmother was very disappointed.

I said 'thank you' to my mother. My mother is very kind and wise. She always gives me good advice. In the future, I might have to live with my husband's parents, so I want to find a man with a nice mother and father!

EIGHT

S san (34) Tokyo

Five years ago, I was working in an office in Tokyo. The job was very hard. We were very busy every day. Some days I didn't have time for lunch. At lunchtimes, I went to the convenience store and got a bento lunchbox and some tea. I ate the bento at my desk while I was working. Then I worked until 10:00pm.

It was a very hard job. I didn't have time to talk to my co-workers very much.

One day, a new staff member joined our section. We had a welcome party for her at a restaurant near my office. Twelve people joined the party. We sat on cushions on the tatami mats. I sat near the door. A man from my section sat next to me. We started talking.

In the office, we were very busy every day, so I didn't have chance to talk to him. But, in the restaurant, we talked a lot. We talked about many things. We talked about our hometowns. He was from Yokohama. We also talked about sports. In university, he was in the kendo club. I didn't like kendo, but I liked sports very much. I was in the tennis club. We talked about our university days.

Then, we talked about our weekends. At that time, I went to the gym every Sunday. I enjoyed using the running machines and going to fitness classes. The man also went to the gym on Sundays. However, he went to a different gym. We talked about fitness and training. I had a really nice time.

After that, in the office, we sometimes talked while we ate our bento at our desks. Then, after a few months, we started to send each other emails from our mobile phones.

Then, one day, we were very busy at work. We worked until 11:00pm.

At 11:00pm, he asked, "Are you hungry?"

I said, "Yes, I am."

He said, "Shall we go for something to eat?"

So we went to a *ramen* noodle shop and we ate *ramen* together. We talked a lot. Then, I looked at my watch. It was 1:00am! We had been talking for two hours!

A few months later, we started dating. Then, after a year, we got married!

All our co-workers were very happy.

Now, we have a daughter. She is one year old. I quit my job and now I am a housewife. We live in Tokyo. I am very happy! I have a nice apartment and a nice family!

THANK YOU

Thank you for reading Women's Konkatsu Tales! We hope you enjoyed it. (Word count: 3,357)

If you enjoyed the book, you might also enjoy the book Men's Konkatsu Tales by I Talk You Talk Press.

If you would like to read more graded readers, please visit our website
http://www.italkyoutalk.com

Other Level 2 graded readers include
Adventure in Rome
Andre's Dream
A Passion for Music
Christmas Tales
Danger in Seattle
Don't Come Back
Finders Keepers…
Marcy's Bakery
Men's Konkatsu Tales
Salaryman Secrets!
Stories for Halloween
The Perfect Wedding
The House in the Forest
The School on Bolt Street

Train Travel
Trouble in Paris

ABOUT THE AUTHOR

I Talk You Talk Press is a Japan-based publisher of language textbooks, graded readers and language learning/teaching resources.

Our team is made up of highly experienced language teachers and translators, who have all studied at least one additional language to an advanced level.

This experience enables us to design our materials from the perspective of both the teacher and the learner. We consult with both teachers and language learners when designing our textbooks and graded readers, and test our materials extensively in the classroom before publication.

We are a fast-growing press, and currently publish graded readers for learners of English. We publish new graded readers monthly.

www.ingramcontent.com/pod-product-compliance
Lightning Source LLC
Chambersburg PA
CBHW032006060426
42449CB00031B/855